AUSONIUS
Three Amusements

AUSONIUS
Three Amusements

Translated by David R. Slavitt

PENN

University of Pennsylvania Press

Philadelphia

Commemoration IV, to Attius Patera, appeared in
Partisan Review, 1998.
"A Nuptial Cento" appeared in *New England Review*, 1998.

10 9 8 7 6 5 4 3 2 1

Published by
University of Pennsylvania Press
Philadelphia, Pennsylvania 19104-4112

Library of Congress Cataloging-in-Publication Data
Ausonius, Decimus Magnus.
[Poems. English. Selections]
Ausonius : three amusements / translated by David R. Slavitt.
   p. cm.
 ISBN-13: 978-0-8122-1953-1
 ISBN-10: 0-8122-1953-8 (pbk. : alk. paper)
  1. Ausonius, Decimus Magnus—Translations into English. 2. Epigrams, Latin—
France—Translations into English. 3. College teachers—France—Bordeaux—
Poetry. 4. Weddings—Poetry. I. Slavitt, David R., 1935– . II. Title.
PA6222.E5S57 1998
871'.01—dc21   980286
                                                                          C

For Charles Ingles, Vera Heideman, Hazel Smith, Jean Godolphin, Ralph Small, Joseph Dodge, Dudley Fitts, Emory Basford, William Holden, William Madsen, Maynard Mack, Charles Fenton, Richard Sewall, Beecher Hogan, Benjamin Nangle, Davis Harding, Cleanth Brooks, Paul Pickerel, Robert Penn Warren, Paul Weiss, Marjorie Nicholson, William Tyndall, Mark Van Doren, James Clifford, and Richard W. B. Lewis

Contents

Introduction

Decimus Magnus Ausonius was born about A.D. 310 in
Bordeaux to Julius Ausonius, a physician, and Aemilia
Aeonia, the daughter of one Caecilius Argicius Ar-
borius. He was educated at Bordeaux and then Tou-
louse, where his maternal uncle Aemilius Magnus Ar-
borius was a professor. When this uncle was summoned
to Constantinople to become tutor to one of the sons of
Constantine, Ausonius accompanied him. He returned
to Bordeaux to continue his studies in rhetoric and be-
came, around A.D. 334, a *grammaticus* (instructor) at the
University of Bordeaux and, later on, a *rhetor* (profes-
sor). After thirty years or so of teaching, he was sum-
moned by Emperor Valentinian I to be the tutor to the
young prince Gratian. When the emperor took Gratian
on the expedition of 368–69 against the Germans, the
tutor came along. This intimate connection with the em-
peror's household resulted in Ausonius' appointment
as *questor sacri palatii*, and when his pupil Gratian suc-
ceeded to the throne, Ausonius' preferment continued.
He became governor of Gaul and eventually consul.

(His family also did well. His father, now nearly ninety, was given the honorary rank of prefect of Illyricum in 375, and the following year his son Hesperius was made proconsul of Africa, which was the first of several increasingly important positions.)

In 383 the army revolted under Maximus, Gratian was murdered at Lyons, and Valentinian II was driven out of Italy. Ausonius returned to Bordeaux and retired from public life, devoting himself to literature and to correspondence with various eminent men, many of whom were his former pupils. In 388 Theodosius overthrew Maximus, but Ausonius seems not to have returned to political activity. Even had he been invited to do so, he may, in his late seventies, have preferred a quiet life on his country estate where he had his writing and the company of his friends. The exact date of his death is not known but it was probably toward the end of 393 or in 394, there being nothing any later from his pen.

He is an elegant, affable, civilized, and witty poet. Clubbable. His most ambitious work is probably the *Mosella*, a performance of nearly five hundred lines about the river that catalogues all the fish that can be found in it and serves as a travelogue, discussing the buildings and the cities along the course of the waterway. What attracted me, however, were his more playful productions. He was an early exemplar of a type I knew back at Yale in the fifties, one of those charming performers at the Elizabethan club about whom one eventually heard that, during the war, he had been one of those who had broken the German naval code, or had been chief of O.S.S. operations in Istanbul. The playfulness they exhibited to us in their puns and jokes was what they'd earned by exertions that hadn't been limited to academic exercises but extended into the real world.

These selections—amusements, really—are mostly from that side of Ausonius' work. The epigrams are graceful and bright. The "Commemorations of the Professors of Bordeaux" is a suave, relaxed, and oddly moving series of reminiscences of his teachers and colleagues. The Cento is a piece of erudite roistering which is impossible to translate but which I have tried to recreate. (My translation has its own preface, where there is an explanation of how it works and what is going on.) All I want to say about it here is that if it is a mark of sophistication to be able to entertain two contradictory ideas at the same time, the Cento is as reliable a test as I know for one's sophistication quotient. What is wonderful about it is that the original Virgilian lines and half lines of which it is composed retain most of their grandeur even as they are put to their new, improbably menial, and thrillingly disgraceful use.

It is, meanwhile, exhilarating and delightful for a writer to know with such serene certainty as this piece provides that if a given reader doesn't like it, it is the reader's fault, surely, and not Ausonius' or mine.

COMMEMORATIONS
OF THE PROFESSORS
OF BORDEAUX

Preface

It is not enough that I think of you often, you gentle
    men
    who were not my kin but as dear to me: my teachers
who shared with me their love of learning and culture
    and Rome.
    I set down, then, on the page what I can
    remember—
as a pious deed from which the young may learn and
    keep
    my ghost in their hearts as I keep yours in mine.

I
Tiberius Victor Minervius, Orator

You, first, Minervius. You were a second Quintillian.
    An ornament yourself, you gave our gown
that grandeur we take on ourselves each day in our
    robing chambers.

Constantinople and Rome you dazzled, and then
our little town where you were our main claim to fame.
   If Calahorra, in Spain, could preen itself
as the great Quintillian's birthplace, we knew that you
     had put us
   on the world's map. Or better, think of the city
that is truly yours, its citizens your pupils, the
     hundreds
   and thousands you gave the courts and the ranks of
     the Senate.
I do not include myself. My ascent to the consulship
   is a strange story I'll tell some other time,
the point, here, being merely that students of yours did
     well.
   I come to praise the master of panegyric,
Isocrates' equal. I come to argue the case of a lawyer
   Quintillian would have respected or even feared.
No easy task, but one I cannot evade. I stroll
   by the banks of a river and look at the turbulent
     water.
I think of your torrent of words, clear except for the
     flecks
   of precious gold shot with dazzles of sunlight.
Your gestures, I remember as reason's ballet, that art
   Demosthenes showed the world, the orator's true

hallmark of greatness, as we who saw you could not
    deny.
    Those natural gifts of your striking looks, your
        commanding
posture, your quickness of mind, your prodigious
    memory . . . these
    I can set down as if in a ledger, but we
who were there can attest our amazement at trivial
    manifestations . . .
    I remember once, in a tavern where we hung out,
a couple of students nearby were occupied with a
    board game
    to which our attention somehow turned, and you
    could recall
every throw of the dice and the moves each player had
    made—
    the whole thing! And you weren't trying and hadn't
been paying special attention. A sweet and gentle man,
    I never heard you say any unkind word,
even in jest. I remember you kept a modest table,
    indulging yourself only on special occasions.
And after six decades, when you died, you left no heir
    but us—I mourned your death as that of a father
or, say, of a young friend, premature and shocking.
    Perhaps, if spirits live, you remember us.

But we remember you, and keep you alive in our best
    moments, for all our achievements are partly yours.

II
Latinus Alcimus Alethius, Rhetorician

Let no one, now or ever, charge me with having failed
    to discharge the debt I owe you, Alcimus. You, too,
I remember as one of the grand men of the old school.
    The great tradition we think of these days with
        longing
and some chagrin, knowing how much we have lost, in
    you
    was living still: from the breath you exhaled we
        knew
what the air had been like in Athens and Rome in her
    greatest days.
    How shall I describe your selfless devotion
to the life of learning? For most young scholars, the
    goad is ambition,
    but success in the hurly burly world outside

your library's narrow windows was nothing for you to
    resist.
    You'd never been tempted. The thought hadn't
    crossed your mind.
To whom in these days can we look for such learning as
    yours and that easy
    but never undignified manner? A person in need
could always come to you—a scholar with some tough
    question,
    or a desperate client others had turned away.
You wrote with a classic restraint but an elegant
    clarity—Julian,
    who held his scepter so briefly, will be remembered
    long
because of your panegyric, and Sallust, the prefect of
    Gaul,
    will endure as much from your pages as his deeds.
And you, too, will defy the forgetfulness of death,
    living on in us, your disciples and students,
whose virtues and talents, we freely admit to the world,
    are yours.
    In our best moments, men of discerning can
    recognize
you, that special grace and style that was all your own.

Is that too fulsome for you? Do these words
violate your standards? I fear that it may be so,
    but the fault is that of my love and gratitude,
for which, O maestro, I know I can count on your
        forgiveness,
    as all of us did so often. We, whom you greatly
enlarged, have been, by your death, diminished and
        now seem normal,
    like other men. We are not. Sweet be your rest.

III
Luciolus, Rhetorician

Of him, my fellow pupil, my tutor, and then my
        colleague,
    of him who was my friend, what can I say?
His intellect and grace ought to have had more time,
    but the fates often begrudge such opulent gifts.
Lachesis snuffed him out like a candle flame and
        extinguished
    brilliance to sudden blackness. He left a son

and daughter, a wife, and a father bereft at their
    grievous loss
  his talents and virtues make all the harder to bear.
Not once did I hear from your mouth, to a slow
    student or servant,
  the least ungentle word. I think of your kindness,
your goodness of heart, and reckon from my own grief
    what they,
  your kinfolk, feel. I pray they may find the strength
and courage to bear this blow. And for you, Ausonius
    prays
  for your elegant spirit's repose: Farewell, old friend.

IV
Attius Patera [Pater], Rhetorician

You, sir, had reached your prime when I was a baby;
  as a very young man, I remember
you were an ancient, venerable, surviving
  to great age from another
and better age. You were my teachers' teacher,

of whom they all still boasted.
They said you had come of a long line of Druids,
    priests of their god Belenus.
Apollo was thus your patron, guide, and protector.
    From him you had your name,
"Patera," the sobriquet of Phoebus' priests.
    Your father Phoebicius, your brother
of the same name, and your son Delphidius all
    bore that deity's blazon
from whom you had your gifts, eloquence, style,
    concision, mellifluousness
your friends and colleagues envied. Your wit was
        gentle,
    your memory, always impressive,
and your learning, vast. Abstemious, modest, precise,
    you were a rare bird—
an old eagle, still strong, still sharp of eye,
    and still gracefully soaring.

V
Attius Tiro Delphidius, Rhetorician

As you followed your father in life, in career and
    talents,
  so, Delphidius, still
do you follow him here in these words of my sorry
    laments,
  this text of tears and praise.
You lisped in numbers, they say, and invented your
    own
  nursery rhymes and songs.
Prodigious, amazing, you wrote as a schoolboy epics
  getting the meters right,
faster than most grown-ups could set down their
    thoughts
  in swaths of workmanlike prose.
A golden boy you were, the son of an eminent father,
  and fame attended you early—
a blessing but not unmixed. You might have preferred
  to sit at your desk in your study
in quiet pursuit of the muse, but clients would seek
    you out
  to appear for them in court,

at this hearing, at that provincial tribunal,
   or even the emperor's bench . . .
Dealing this way with powerful people, one
   can engender powerful hatreds.
In precincts so full of dangers, envy and enmity
    schemed,
   conniving to bring you down.
Their attempt was a failure. Your father's sorrowful
    pleading
   won you a full pardon.
Changed, embittered, diminished, you turned then to
    teaching,
   but your heart never was in it.
One by one, your pupils' parents withdrew
   their dunderhead darlings.
You gave it up at last. And from time to time
   you or your ghost appeared
to exchange greetings and hurry off somewhere . . .
   You died young and were spared
the shame of your wife's execution, the pain of your
    daughter's
   perverse and depressing end.
Still, I remember you young, that hope, those gifts,
   that damnably brilliant promise . . .

VI
Alethius Minervius, Son of Delphidius, Rhetorician

O you fair blossom
of youth, and the fond
hope of your father's bosom,
where have you gone?

Precocious, you were,
at a schoolboy's age,
running a seminar,
a smooth-cheeked sage.

Your father's equal
we called you then,
and even your grandfather's sequel.
Most learned of men,

he taught at Rome
in their marbled halls,
while you were content to stay home
with your old pals,

where you could attend
the hearts and minds
of the cohort that called you their friend.
Fortune's designs

are strange indeed,
or clear and cruel.
We refuse to learn to read
in her hard school

those somber lessons
of how she will make
loans, and not outright presents,
and is liable to take

everything back,
turning the sheen
of that brilliance you had to black.
It's sordid and mean,

how your father's woes
blighted your life,
but that's how it sometimes goes.
Your lovely wife

upped and left.
At first you were numb,
then absolutely bereft.
We were struck dumb

by your explication
of Virgil's line,[1]
a too vivid demonstration
of how in time

the green grass
of summer must fade,
as it did for Marcellus, alas.
It is also said

by Horace somewhere[2]
that nothing is wholly
blessed. It isn't fair,
but we learn, slowly.

1. *Aen.* vi. 869
2. *Odes* II. xvi 27f.

VII
Leontius, called Lascivus, Grammarian

It wasn't true
what they said about you,
and all of us knew,
whenever we spoke
of Horny Leon,
it was just a joke
that was handed down
and still went around,
absurd and unkind,
although you didn't mind.
And now you are gone,
a teacher we miss.
A bit of a priss
you were: it was this
that started some boy
who was out to annoy
or distract you in class.
Now nothing, alas,
no matter how crude,
will provoke you or try
your patience, as I

refer, one last time,
with a feeling of shame
to your old nickname
that we used to your face
and you took in good grace.
This deplorable rhyme
is to honor, dear sir,
that kind scholar you were.

VIII
The Greek Grammarians of Bordeaux

"The soul is deathless," we used to read
on the first page of a Greek text.
And I hope it's true, as I come to speak
    of which of you, next . . .

Romulus, Corinthius,
Sperchius, or else his son
Menesthius, our patient masters
    back in Greek One?

How to memorialize those men
under whose discipline we learned
to elaborate a verb's conjugation?
    The night oil burned,

as, after a while, we did, ourselves,
with appreciation and love for what
they drilled into our heads and we
    never forgot.

A thankless task it was, but now
I offer those thanks belatedly,
knowing how much we owe to them.
    Their memory

is ever fresh with us. May earth
lie lightly on them in their rest.
With all of us for whom they labored,
    their names are blessed.

IX

Jucundus, Grammarian of Bordeaux,
Brother of Leontius

Some said you'd lost it: others more
severe maintained you'd never even had it.
To hell with them, Jucundus. For
your charm and kindness, I give you credit.
Your limitations you confessed.
You weren't the brightest but one of the best.

X

To the Latin Grammarians, Macrinus,
Sucuro, Concordius, Phoebicius, and
Ammonius, Scholars of Bordeaux,
and Anastasius of Poitiers

Let me recall
them one and all,
those modest men

from whom we got
our love of letters.
We boys were not
impressed back then.
Now we know better.
Macrinus taught
amo, amas,
amat . . . It wasn't
ever pleasant,
but someone's got
to take that class.

Sucuro, then,
and Concordius,
(gentle men,
both) molded us.
I'm afraid it was
barely a living.
Nonetheless, you
kept on with it, giving
great riches to
us yokels who
in part repay
our debt to you
by passing on

those lessons to others
whom we in turn
are teaching today,
now that you're gone.
In the chairs we sat in
trying to learn,
our younger brothers
study Latin.

Phoebicius was
an aristocrat,
well groomed, though running
somewhat to fat.
He was always punning.
Ammonius
was a bully, a brute,
we held in very
low repute.
And yet I would keep
the name alive
of an adversary
who now lies mute.

And Anastasius? I have dim
but pleasant recollections of him.

He went away
to teach at Poitiers
in a poor post that barely fed
and clothed the man.
And now he's dead,
but let us recall
as well as we can
him and the rest
who did their best
and bless them all.

XI
Herculanus, My Nephew, Grammarian
of Bordeaux

Herculanus, kinsman, as a scholar you
promised so much, but what did it come to?
After that first blossoming, no fruits . . .
You discovered other, more lively pursuits.
With such great gifts, you were deserving of far
better things than to be the one in the bar

of whom men said that, before you fell off your stool,
you had been one of the brightest in our school.

XII
Thalassus, Latin Grammarian of Bordeaux

And who remembers you? Alas, not I,
but the older students said that in years gone by
Thalassus . . . What? I cannot bring it back.
Only your name, that fragment. The rest is black.
But you were a teacher here, and I must try, sir,
to do what little I can, as I wish you good-bye, sir.

XIII
Citarius, Sicilian of Syracuse, Greek Grammarian at Bordeaux

Of you, dear friend what
can one say in such dismal
times? In the old days,

you'd have had the fame
of Aristarchus, say, or
of Zenodotus,

eminent men, those
Alexandrian scholars.
You could write verses

surpassing in grace
those of Simonides of
Ceos. Any praises

I cobble and patch
together will fall far short
of what you deserve.

From Syracuse, you
came to our city and made it
a far better place,

a home of the arts
and a center of learning.
You married quite well,

a woman well-bred
and with money, too. But Fate
denied you offspring.

We were your children,
and honor and love you for
your gifts and friendship.

XIV
Censorius Atticus Agricius, Rhetorician

Those Byzantines who spend so much time and energy
    making
        seating plans and figuring who should precede

whom would disapprove of my having waited till now
   to memorialize you, one of the foremost
speakers of our day—but you are by no means
    forgotten.
   For the dead, I think, there is neither rank nor time,
and all tribute, early or late, that echoes forever,
   is welcome—as on our library shelves, the books
of ancient and recent authors jostle in comradely
    fashion
   with no respect for time. Nobly born,
you graced your eminent chair in this Athens of Gaul,
   that Nazarius held once and famous Patera,
with talent and breeding, too. Your wife and your
    children mourn
   your loss as do we all at your family tomb.

XV
Nepotianus, Grammarian and Rhetorician

A dear man, whose lively wit
was always kind and gentle, it
is sad to think that you are gone,

whom all of us depended on
for your wise counsel. Others could
offer suggestions almost as good,
but to which of them would we have turned?
You, with your discretion, earned
our trust, our love and gratitude.
Abstemious in both drink and food,
you were our teacher, guide, comrade,
alike in happy times and sad.
Cleanthes' equal in grace, you knew
the speeches of Scaurus and Probus too
by heart and could, if asked, recite,
instilling in our hearts delight
in oratory. Ninety years
you lived and thrived. Now we shed tears
for the children and kinfolk at your wake,
but also for our own sorrow's sake,
for those of us whom you have left
behind enriched, now feel bereft.

XVI
Aemilius Magnus Arborius,
Rhetorician of Toulouse

You, I praise under double obligation,
for you were both rhetorician and also my uncle.
All pieties combine—my respect for kin,
for calling, and for place. We flowered here:
Arborius, my grandfather, my father
of the same name, and you, my uncle, who sprang
from Aeduan stock. Your mother came from Dax.
Hard work, talent, breeding, and luck all joined
together to give you a life of comfort and honor.
You had a chair, you had an opulent house,
a noble wife, and the friendship of all the great
and clever men of Toulouse. Your reputation
resonated in Thrace, in Constantinople,
which summoned you at length, and as tutor to Caesar,
you were master to the master of all the world.
And there you died, not old. Your parents mourned
        you.
The August prince, as a sign of his great favor,
returned your body here to the family tomb,

where every year we assemble to do you honor
and remember you this day, in pride and sorrow.

XVII
Exuperius, Rhetorician of Toulouse

Your eloquence, man, was matchless, beyond all reason,
or, say without any reason. But all the purer,
flights of clouds on the wind, storms without rain
or lightning in the bowl of the high sky,
furious demonstrations of syntax, sheerest
persiflage and rodomontade to perplex
and amaze with gestures no one had seen before
and no sane man has attempted since. I salute you
thirty-two ways to Thursday and your cascades
of words, your singular gifts. In Toulouse you started,
but what did they know in Toulouse? How could they
    ever
appreciate such a nonpareil? You removed
to Narbonne where you tutored the sons of the great
    Dalmatius

(Strangely believe it!). They grew up and later made
    you
a governor in Spain, which somehow survived
your death. Such things can happen. I include
your name with a straight face, almost. You were ours,
a Bordeaux rhetorician—and who can deny it?

XVIII
Marcellus, Son of Marcellus,
Grammarian of Narbonne

A wretched boyhood: a harridan mother drove you
away from your home and city, but stepmother
    Fortune
smiled on that charming waif that you must have been,
restoring all you'd lost and giving you more:
a home in Narbonne, a nobly born young woman
to be your wife, and classrooms full of the sons
of the best people. You then were rich and famous . . .
I think of you that way, at that fine moment
before it went bad and, disgraced and ruined, you
    lost it

all. Or not quite all. The learning remained,
yours and your students'. No one could take that away,
and I will not omit your name: you were one of us.

XIX
Sedatus, Rhetorican of Toulouse

You went away to Toulouse, where you married and
        taught
and prospered, but you were from here, and learned at
        these desks
and benches the skills of our calling. I must not forget
        you,
a flower of this great garden, nourished by soil
as rich as any in all the world. Your sons
are also scholars and, teaching in Narbonne and Rome,
maintain our great tradition. Is it Fortune's whim?
The light? The lay of the land? Or the happy chance
of like-minded men in one place and time, enriched
by one another's example and friendship? Bordeaux
lived wherever you were and shared in your fame.
In pride, I salute you sir: you did us proud.

XX
Staphylius, Rhetorician, Native of Auch

You sir, were not from here, did not even teach here.
    But rules are made to be broken, and you were kind,
a kind of uncle, a gentle friend, and a learned man
    whose name I set down with affection. Syntactical
        knots
you could unravel with ease, but you also excelled in
        other
    subjects—history, law. The writings of Livy
and Varro you knew, and Herodotus, too. Your tongue
        was persuasive,
    but purest gold was your heart. I remember you old,
distinguished, speaking in measured cadence, and
        showing us youngsters
    what life could be for a man of wisdom and faith.
A stranger to anger as well as to grief, you maintained a
        decorous
    grace to the end of your properly peaceful days.

XXI
Crispus and Urbicus, Greek and Latin Grammarians

Crispus, you
deserve mention, too,
working away
day after day
teaching the A,
B, C to the first
classes — the worst
job there is
in the teaching biz.
True or not,
with a beer and a shot
you could get through
the day and would do
this scut-work, although
it was said you could write
splendid verses at night,
like Virgil's or,
say, Horace's. Poor
fellow, I do

suppose it was true,
and a kind of a curse
that made life even worse.
And Urbicus, you,
who were talented too,
could not have had fun
teaching Greek One,
but at the day's end
with Crispus, your friend,
in the firelight
you'd recover, recite
from Homer, who soothes
with his beauties and truths
those who,
like you two,
are treated unfairly
and get along barely
on patience and nerve.
You were quite a pair.
It is most unfair,
we know, and yet
how few men get
what they deserve.

XXII
Victorius, Adjunct, or Private Docent

What didn't you know? A repository of odd
and obscure texts, you preferred to unroll old scrolls
than to read what your colleagues were talking about
    in commons.
But now and again, you'd pipe up from your end of the
    table
with just the right morsel of information—the code
of the pontifex held this, or the treaty of Whatsis
provided thus and so. The order of kings
of countries no one remembered, you had at hand
and could rattle off—but only if asked to do so.
The ancient rules of the priesthood, you could recite,
or Solon's laws or Draco's, and how they applied
and with what exceptions in this circumstance or
    that . . .
It was all in your head. If the rest of us knew Virgil's
poems or Cicero's speeches, you were the master
of all abstruse, arcane, and bizarre information.
Everything there was to know, you'd have learned,
if Lachesis had not dispatched you on that last journey.

You should have been richer and better known. I
    inscribe
your name in pious tribute, hoping your shade,
if you have one and if it can feel, may perhaps be
    pleased.

XXIII
Dynamius of Bordeaux, Who Taught and
Died in Spain

I will not leave you out, sir. You grew up, studied here,
and argued here in the courts, until that woeful
business with the Lord Mayor's wife . . . You fled
to Spain somewhere—Lerida, I think—and assumed
another name, Flavinius. You married
money, and thrived and prospered there. Years passed,
and you came back to Bordeaux, but nothing you saw
was what you remembered. So many you'd loved or
    hated
or feared were dead. There were no ties left to hold
    you,

so you went back to end your days in the lazy
Lerida sunshine. Happy? Sad? Who knows?
At peace, I prefer to think, as I hope you are now
at peace. What is real in space and time but friendship?
From far-away and long-ago, I salute you
and send what solace affection may bring your spirit.

XXIV
Acilius Glabrio, the Younger,
of Bordeaux, Grammarian

We were students together, and then you were my
    pupil,
and then we were colleagues: I taught rhetoric, you
led the way for youngsters through grammar's tangles
    and thickets.
Yours was a distinguished house. Your father Acilinus
was the son of the great Dardanus. Cheerful and kind,
unfailingly polite to all, you enjoyed
farming your family's lands, and you studied and
    taught

and deserved a long, tranquil, and decorous life . . .
And suddenly you are gone, and your wife and
      children
and parents mourn the husband, father, and son
so abruptly snatched away. With them, I mourn,
as I ask myself those questions we tried to avoid:
What is it all about? And how do we bear it?

XXV
Conclusion

You who may read this, know that these
were teachers here. An honorable calling.
Some were great, some were okay.
They did the best they could. They are all
dead now, and I recall them
in piety and with thanks. They deserve
at the least that their names on living breath
be shouted aloud into the air,
as if from the schoolyard over which
they looked with greater or lesser patience

during recess. The last bell
has sounded for them, but its echo lingers,
albeit faintly. Listen hard.
You hear it or feel it. Enriching us all,
these men, together, were Bordeaux's glory.

XXVI
The Poet's Farewell

A last valedictory word or two
for these men of words who studied and taught,
some of them famous and some obscure.
Now that they are gone, we ought
to pay them homage, for their sakes—
if their souls can hear what we say or feel—
but for our own as well, whose debts
and loves were great. These tears are real.
I pray your ashes may lie secure
and your memory last. O gentle men,
if some of the myths we studied are true,
in another world we may meet again.

A NUPTIAL CENTO

Translator's Preface: A Letter to Henry and Sarah Taylor

Dear Sarah, dear Henry,

In Ausonius' prefatory letter to his friend Paulus, he offers an explanation for what he calls "a trifling and worthless little book which no effort has shaped or pains have polished," and he justifies the mediocrity of the production with the excuse that the Emperor Valentinian, having produced such a poem, suggested (i.e., commanded) that Ausonius do one, too, producing a similar work on a similar subject—a wedding. It was a delicate predicament, because he didn't want to outshine the emperor, but neither did he want to be altogether outshone. "This book, then, composed rapidly in a single day with some lamp-lit hours added," was what he produced. It was, as he admits, "a task for memory only, which has to gather up scattered tags and integrate mangled scraps together."

Ausonius sets out the rules of the game for making a "cento,"[1] a poem "completely constructed from a variety of passages" of something else and meaning something

1. The word comes either from κέντων, a Greek word meaning to plant slips of trees, or perhaps from κεντόνη or κεντονάρων, which were words meaning a patchwork garment. A cento, in any event, is a poem composed of fragments of another poet's work.

different. Ideally, one puts together half lines, or to one line with the following half one finds a different concluding half line that seems to fit. To put two whole lines together is weak, and to have three in succession is fundamentally to admit defeat. The break point of the line ought to be at the caesura.[2]

"The game . . . is to harmonize different meanings, to make the pieces arbitrarily connected seem naturally related, to let foreign elements show no chink of light between them, to prevent the widely disparate from proclaiming the violence by which they were joined together, the crammed from bulging excessively, the loosely knit from falling apart."

The attempt is to be, at the same time, suave and comic, to have fun with the basic text (in Ausonius' case, the work of Virgil) without being disrespectful of it. One must remember that for the Emperor Valentinian and for Ausonius there weren't concordances and hypertext engines. They may have consulted a manuscript now and then to check a word or a phrase, but they constructed their patchwork pieces from what they had in their heads.

To do a translation of Ausonius' cento, one could put together Virgilian phrases, but the shock of recognition of those phrases in new contexts would be lost to those

2. "Caesura" is, bizarrely enough, the word on your license plate.

who didn't already know Virgil well. The ideal reader would also have most of Virgil committed to memory, and of course this would be in Latin. For such readers, there is no need for a translation into English.

More entertaining and more useful, I thought, would be to follow the instructions, to take an English author —Shakespeare is our Virgil, surely—and find lines and half-lines with which one could more or less follow the narrative line of Ausonius' naughty poem.

That you two are getting married just at the moment when I am working on (or playing with) this frivolous project seems a coincidence too delightful to ignore. I am relieved to have a couple to whom I can dedicate this, secure in the knowledge that they will take it the right way, overlooking its grossness (which is part of the game) and interpreting it as I intend, and, I am sure, as Ausonius also intended, as an elaborate if complicated compliment.

As he says in his letter to his friend, you can, at the very worst, snip the phrases apart again and restore them to their original home, in your Complete Shakespeare, where they will no longer seem offensive or obscene and where they will grace your household from their honored place on the bookshelf.

Valete,

David

I
Praefatio

Accipite haec animis laetasque advertite mentes,[1]
ambo animis, ambo insignes praestantibus armis;[2]
ambo florentes,[3] genus insuperabile bello.[4]
tuque prior,[5] nam te maioribus ire per altum
auspiciis manifesta fides,[6] quo iustior alter
nec pietate fuit, nec bello maior et armis;[7]
tuque puerque tuus,[8] magnae spes altera Romae,[9]
flos veterum virtusque virum,[10] mea maxima cura,[11]
nomine avum referens, animo manibusque parentem.[12]
non iniussa cano.[13] sua cuique exorsa laborem
fortunamque ferent:[14] mihi iussa capessere fas est.[15]

1. *Aen.* v. 304.
2. *Aen.* xi. 291
3. *Ecl.* vii. 4.
4. *Aen.* iv. 40.
5. *Aen.* vi. 834.
6. *Aen.* iii. 374f.
7. *Aen.* i. 544f.
8. *Aen.* iv. 94.
9. *Aen.* xii. 168.
10. *Aen.* viii. 500.
11. *Aen.* i. 678.
12. *Aen.* xii. 348.
13. *Ecl.* vi. 9.
14. *Aen.* x. 111f.
15. *Aen.* i. 77.

I
Preface

Friends, Romans, countrymen,[1] I greet thy love.[2]
Bestow upon the eyes of this young couple,[3]
that twixt heaven and earth[4] hangs weights upon
my tongue,[5] fairest boding dreams.[6] A thousand
    thousand
blessings.[7] Who deserves greatness?[8] O noble fellow,[9]
worthy of this noble wife,[10] with present grace
and great prediction,[11] see your guests approach[12]
that give sweet tidings of the sun's uprise.[13]
I tender you,[14] mine ancient friend,[15] my thoughts

1. *Julius Caesar* III, 2.
2. *Othello* III, 3.
3. *Tempest* IV, 1.
4. *Winter's Tale* V, l.
5. *As You Like It* I, 2.
6. *Richard III* V, 3.
7. *Henry VIII* V, 5.
8. *Coriolanus* I, 1.
9. *Coriolanus* I, 4.
10. *Julius Caesar* II, 1.
11. *Macbeth* I, 3.
12. *Winter's Tale* IV, 4.
13. *Titus Andronicus* III, 1.
14. *Richard III* II, 4.
15. *Timon of Athens* V, 2.

II
Cena Nuptialis

Expectata dies aderat[1] dignisque hymenaeis[2]
matres atque viri,[3] iuvenes ante ora parentum[4]
conveniunt stratoque super discumbitur ostro.
dant famuli manibus lymphas[5] onerantque canistris
dona laboratae Cereris[6] pinguisque ferinae[7]
viscera tosta ferunt.[8] series longissima rerum:[9]
alituum pecudumque genus[10] capreaeque sequaces[11]

1. *Aen.* v. 104.
2. *Aen.* xi. 355.
3. *Aen.* vi. 306.
4. *Georg.* iv. 477.
5. *Aen.* i. 700f.
6. *Aen.* viii. 180.
7. *Aen.* i. 215.
8. *Aen.* viii. 180.
9. *Aen.* i. 641.
10. *Aen.* viii. 27.
11. *Georg.* ii. 374.

that are whirled like a potter's wheel.[16] By cock and pie,
    sir,[17]
I tender you my service, such as it is.[18]

II
The Marriage Feast

The kitchen malkin pins her richest lockram
'bout her reechy neck.[1] What time we will
our celebration keep,[2] all full with feasting
on your sight![3] That I profess myself
in banqueting, give me twenty cunning cooks.[4]
I would have all well betwixt you.[5] Our carnations
and streak'd gillyvors[6] proclaim your love
and honor,[7] love, i' faith, to the very tip

16. *1st part Henry VI* I, 5.
17. *2nd part Henry IV* V, 1.
18. *Richard II* II, 3.

1. *Coriolanus* II, 1.
2. *Twelfth Night* IV, 3.
3. Sonnet LXXV.
4. *Romeo and Juliet* IV, 2.
5. *King Lear* II, 4.
6. *Winter's Tale* IV, 3.
7. *Macbeth* I, 4.

non absunt illic[12] neque oves haedique petulci[13]
et genus aequoreum,[14] dammae cervique fugaces:[15]
ante oculos interque manus sunt[16] mitia poma.[17]

    Postquam exempta fames et amor compressus
      edendi,[18]
crateras magnos statuunt[19] Bacchumque ministrant.[20]
sacra canunt,[21] plaudunt choreas et carmina dicunt.[22]
nec non Thraeicius longa cum veste sacerdos
obloquitur numeris septem discrimina vocum.[23]
at parte ex alia[24] biforem dat tibia cantum.[25]
omnibus una quies operum,[26] cunctique relictis
consurgunt mensis:[27] per limina laeta frequentes,[28]
discurrunt variantque vices[29] populusque patresque,[30]

12. *Georg.* ii. 471.
13. *Georg.* iv. 10.
14. *Georg.* iii. 243.
15. *Georg.* iii. 539.
16. *Aen.* xi. 311.
17. *Ecl.* i. 80.
18. *Aen.* viii. 184.
19. *Aen.* i. 724.
20. *Aen.* viii. 181.
21. *Aen.* ii. 239.
22. *Aen.* vi. 644.
23. *Aen.* vi. 645f.
24. *Aen.* x. 362.
25. *Aen.* ix. 618.
26. *Georg.* iv. 184.
27. *Aen.* viii. 109f.
28. *Aen.* i. 707.
29. *Aen.* ix. 164.
30. *Aen.* ix. 192.

of the nose.[8] We drink this health to you.[9] Myself,
I'll dedicate[10] with a butt of sack,[11] and dainties
to taste,[12] the soul of bounty.[13] Then shall be cakes
and ale,[14] and fancy bred,[15] and what strange fish,[16]
chew'd swallow'd and digested.[17] O my friends![18]
This is not yet an Alexandrian feast![19]
What say you to a piece of beef and mustard?[20]
Proceed by swallowing that,[21] if it shall please you,[22]
and supply it with one gender of herbs or distract it
with many.[23] A good digestion to you all.[24]
And let the pebbles on the hungry beach[25]
envy your great deservings and good name![26]
Wish we all joy and honor.[27] Repose in fame.[28]

8. *Troilus and Cressida* III, 1.
9. *Pericles* II, 3.
10. *Cymbeline* V, 1.
11. *Tempest* II, 2.
12. *Venus and Adonis*, l. 164.
13. *Timon of Athens* I, 2.
14. *Twelfth Night* III, 3.
15. *Merchant of Venice* III, 2.
16. *Tempest* II, 1.
17. *Henry V*, II, 2.
18. *Timon of Athens* I, 2.
19. *Antony and Cleopatra* II, 7.
20. *Taming of the Shrew* IV, 3.
21. *Cymbeline* III, 5.
22. *Hamlet* III, 2.
23. *Othello*, I, 3.
24. *Henry VIII* I, 4.
25. *Coriolanus* V, 3.
26. *1st part Henry IV* IV, 3.
27. *Coriolanus* II, 2.
28. *Titus Andronicus* I, 1.

matronae, pueri,[31] vocemque per ampla volutant
atria: dependent lychni laquearibus aureis.[32]

III
Descriptio Egredientis Sponsae

Tandem progreditur [1] Veneris iustissima cura,[2]
iam matura viro, iam plenis nublis annis,[3]
virginis os habitumque gerens,[4] cui plurimus ignem
subiecit rubor et calefacta per ora cucurrit,[5]
intentos volvens oculos,[6] uritque videndo.[7]
illam omnis tectis agrisque effusa iuventus
turbaque miratur matrum.[8] vestigia primi
alba pedis,[9] dederatque comam diffundere ventis.[10]

---

31. *Aen.* xi. 476.
32. *Aen.* i. 725f.

---

1. *Aen.* iv. 136.
2. *Aen.* x. 132.
3. *Aen.* vii. 53.
4. *Aen.* i. 315.
5. *Aen.* xii. 65f.
6. *Aen.* vii. 251.
7. *Georg.* iii. 215.
8. *Aen.* vii. 812f.
9. *Aen.* v. 566f.
10. *Aen.* i. 319.

III
The Bridal Portrait

What's here? The portrait[1] of her body and beauty[2]
as gives satiety fresh appetite.[3]
Eternity is in her lips and eyes,[4]
nor is not her nose neither nothing.[5] I sing[6]
the pretty dimples of her chin and cheek.[7]
And now, in another part of the field,[8] we come
to her woman's breasts[9] that make wolves howl[10] and
    entrap
the hearts of men,[11] her excellent white bosom[12]

1. *Merchant of Venice* II, 9.
2. *Othello* IV, 1.
3. *Othello* II, 1.
4. *Antony and Cleopatra* I, 3.
5. *Twelfth Night* IV, 1.
6. *Love's Labor's Lost* I, 2.
7. *Winter's Tale* II, 3.
8. *Julius Caesar* V, 3.
9. *Macbeth* I, 5.
10. *Tempest* I, 2.
11. *Merchant of Venice* III, 2.
12. *Hamlet* II, 2.

fert picturatas auri subtemine vestes,[11]
ornatus Argivae Helenae:[12] qualisque videri
caelicolis et quanta solet[13] Venus aurea contra,[14]
talis erat species,[15] talem se laeta ferebat[16]
ad soceros[17] solioque alte subnixa resedit.[18]

IV
Descriptio Egredientis Sponsi

At parte ex alia[1] foribus sese intulit altis[2]
ora puer prima signans intonsa iuventa,[3]
pictus acu[4] chlamydem auratam, quam plurima circum
purpura maeandro duplici Meliboea cucurrit,[5]

11. *Aen.* iii. 483.
12. *Aen.* i. 650.
13. *Aen.* ii. 591f.
14. *Aen.* x. 16.
15. *Aen.* vi. 208.
16. *Aen.* i. 503.
17. *Aen.* ii. 457.
18. *Aen.* i. 506.

---

1. *Aen.* x. 362.
2. *Aen.* xi. 36.
3. *Aen.* ix. 181.
4. *Aen.* ix. 582.
5. *Aen.* v. 250f.

touching the which makes blessed the rude hand.[13]
And 'sblood, I would my face were in her belly.[14]
Her fine foot, straight leg and quivering thigh, [15]
but I have not seen the most [16] and dare not say [17]
but princely shall be their usage, every way.[18]

IV
Portrait of the Groom

He has lived too long on the almsbasket of words! [1]
And yet, of his leg, the manner of his gait,
the expressure [2] . . . tut, I have work enough.[3]
With eyes severe and beard of formal cut,[4]
and his hat penthouse-like o'er the shop of his eyes [5]

13. *Romeo and Juliet* I, 5.
14. *1st part Henry IV*, III, 2.
15. *Romeo and Juliet* II, 1.
16. *Cymbeline* I, 4.
17. *Two Gentlemen of Verona* V, 4.
18. *Titus Andronicus* I, 1.

1. *Coriolanus* V, 6.
2. *Twelfth Night* II, 3.
3. *Titus Andronicus* V, 2.
4. *As You Like It* II, 7
5. *Love's Labor's Lost* III, 1.

et tunicam, molli mater quam neverat auro:[6]
os umerosque deo similis[7] lumenque iuventae.[8]
qualis, ubi oceani perfusus Lucifer unda[9]
extulit os sacrum caelo:[10] sic ora ferebat,[11]
sic oculos[12] cursuque amens ad limina tendit.[13]
illum turbat amor figitque in virgine vultus;[14]
oscula libavit[15] dextramque amplexus inhaesit.[16]

V

Oblatio Munerum

Incedunt pueri pariterque ante ora parentum[1]
dona ferunt,[2] pallam signis auroque rigentem,[3]

6. *Aen.* x. 818.
7. *Aen.* i. 589.
8. *Aen.* i. 590.
9. *Aen.* viii. 589.
10. *Aen.* viii. 591.
11. *Aen.* iii. 490.
12. *Aen.* iii. 490.
13. *Aen.* ii. 321.
14. *Aen.* xii. 70.
15. *Aen.* i. 256.
16. *Aen.* viii. 124.

1. *Aen.* v. 553.
2. *Aen.* v. 101.
3. *Aen.* i. 648.

that with all praise I point at.[6] He hath nimble
spirits in the arteries,[7] and yet his jest is dry [8]
as he is too,[9] by gar.[10] No pedascule,[11]
he bears in his visage [12] such spirits and fires [13] . . .
She will a handmaid be to his desires.[14]

V

The Wedding Gifts

God give you joy, sir, of your gallant bride [1]
as you bear these tokens home,[2] gifts of rich value,[3]

6. *Coriolanus* II, 1.
7. *Love's Labor's Lost* IV, 3.
8. *Love's Labor's Lost* V, 2.
9. *As You Like It* I, 2.
10. *Merry Wives of Windsor* I, 4.
11. *Taming of the Shrew* III, 1.
12. *Twelfth Night* III, 2.
13. *Troilus and Cressida* V, 1.
14. *Titus Andronicus* I, 1.

---

1. *Titus Andronicus* I, 1.
2. *King John* IV, 2.
3. *Merchant of Venice* II, 9.

munera portantes aurique eborisque talenta
et sellam[4] et pictum croceo velamen acantho,[5]
ingens argentum mensis[6] colloque monile
bacatum et duplicem gemmis auroque coronam.[7]
olli serva datur[8] geminique sub ubere nati:[9]
quattuor huic iuvenes[10] totidem innuptaeque puellae:[11]
omnibus in morem tonsa coma;[12] pectore summo
flexilis obtorti per collum circulus auri.[13]

4. *Aen.* xi. 333.
5. *Aen.* i. 711.
6. *Aen.* i. 640.
7. *Aen.* i. 654f.
8. *Aen.* v. 284.
9. *Aen.* v. 285.
10. *Aen.* x. 518.
11. *Aen.* ii. 238.
12. *Aen.* v. 556.
13. *Aen.* v. 558f.

ignorant baubles,[4] base appliances,[5]
green earthen pots,[6] and such immoment toys[7]
as wear the print of our remembrance[8]
who cannot contain our urine for affection,[9]
a love that makes breath poor and speech unable.[10]
This 'tis to be married! this 'tis to have linen,[11]
fine linen, Turkey cushions boss'd with pearl,[12]
and the spoons will be bigger sir.[13] As pigeons bill,
so wedlock would be nibbling.[14] Gold bides still.[15]

4. *Cymbeline* III, 1.
5. *Measure for Measure* III, 1.
6. *Romeo and Juliet* V, 1.
7. *Antony and Cleopatra* V, 2.
8. *Cymbeline* II, 2.
9. *Merchant of Venice* IV, 1.
10. *King Lear* I, 1.
11. *Merry Wives of Windsor* III, 5.
12. *Taming of the Shrew* II, 1.
13. *Henry VIII* V, 4.
14. *As You Like It* III, 3.
15. *Comedy of Errors* II, 1

VI
Epithalamium Utrique

Tum studio effusae matres[1] ad limina ducunt;[2]
at chorus aequalis,[3] pueri innuptaeque puellae,[4]
versibus incomptis ludunt[5] et carmina dicunt:[6]
"O digno coniuncta viro,[7] gratissima coniunx,[8]
sis felix,[9] primos Lucinae experta labores[10]
et mater. cape Maeonii carchesia Bacchi.[11]
sparge, marite, nuces;[12] cinge haec altaria vitta,[13]
flos veterum virtusque virum:[14] tibi ducitur uxor,[15]
omnes ut tecum meritis pro talibus annos
exigat et pulchra faciat te prole parentem.[16]

1. *Aen.* xii. 131.
2. *Aen.* x. 117.
3. *Georg.* iv. 460.
4. *Aen.* vi. 307.
5. *Georg.* ii. 386.
6. *Aen.* vi. 644.
7. *Ecl.* viii. 32.
8. *Aen.* x. 607.
9. *Aen.* i. 330.
10. *Georg.* iv. 340.
11. *Georg.* iv. 380.
12. *Ecl.* viii. 30.
13. *Ecl.* viii. 64.
14. *Aen.* viii. 500.
15. *Ecl.* viii. 29.
16. *Aen.* i. 74f.

VI
Epithalamion

The holy vows of heaven,[1] God keep unbroke.[2]
I'll rhyme you so[3] ten thousand years together[4]
of dinners and suppers and sleeping hours.[5] Go to,
a bargain made.[6] Wherefore rejoice.[7] Soft beds,
sweet words . . .[8] Sound trumpets, sackbuts, psalteries,
and fifes,[9] nor let the fiddler forbear[10]
that hugs his kicky-wicky here at home.[11]
Fetch thee new nuts,[12] and make merry withal.[13]
In bare ruined choirs,[14] let the birds fly,[15]
my pretty chickens[16] that sing a-down a-down.[17]

1. *Hamlet* I, 3.
2. *Richard II* IV, 1.
3. *As You Like It* III, 2.
4. *Winter's Tale* III, 2.
5. *As You Like It* III, 2.
6. *Troilus and Cressida* III, 2.
7. *Julius Caesar* I, 1.
8. *Cymbeline* V, 3.
9. *Coriolanus* V, 4.
10. *Taming of the Shrew* III, 1.
11. *All's Well that Ends Well* II, 3.
12. *Midsummer Night's Dream* IV, 1.
13. *Taming of the Shrew* V, 1.
14. Sonnet LXXIII.
15. *Hamlet* III, 4.
16. *Macbeth* IV, 3.
17. *Hamlet* IV, 5.

fortunati ambo,[17] si quid pia numina possunt,[18]
vivite felices." [19] dixerunt "currite" fusis
concordes stabili fatorum numine Parcae.[20]

VII
Ingressus in Cubiculum

Postquam est in thalami pendentia pumice tecta
perventum,[1] licito tandem sermone fruuntur.[2]
congressi iungunt dextras[3] stratisque reponunt.[4]
at Cytherea novas artes[5] et pronuba Iuno[6]
sollicitat suadetque ignota lacessere bella.[7]
ille ubi complexu[8] molli fovet atque repente

17. *Aen.* ix. 446.
18. *Aen.* iv. 382.
19. *Aen.* iii. 493.
20. *Ecl.* iv. 46f.

---

1. *Georg.* iv. 374f.
2. *Aen.* viii. 468.
3. *Aen.* viii. 467.
4. *Aen.* iv. 392.
5. *Aen.* i. 657.
6. *Aen.* iv. 166.
7. *Aen.* xi. 254.
8. *Aen.* i. 715.

O heavens, can you hear a good man groan?[18]
Why should he stay whom love doth press to go?[19]
And if it please you, so; if not, why, so.[20]

VII
Entry into the Bedchamber

Go we to[1] your bed-chamber,[2] to bed,[3]
the bed of blessed marriage.[4] Eftsoons, I'll tell thee,[5]
sick-thoughted Venus[6] governs our desires.[7]
We make ourselves fools, to disport ourselves[8]
flowing and swelling o'er with arts and exercise,[9]
feat and affectedly.[10] Come, let me clutch thee . . .[11]

18. *Titus Andronicus* IV, 1.
19. *Midsummer Night's Dream* III, 2.
20. *Two Gentlemen of Verona* II, 1.

---

1. *Coriolanus* I, 9.
2. *Richard III* I, 2.
3. *Hamlet* III, 2.
4. *Henry V* V, 2.
5. *Pericles* V, 1.
6. *Venus and Adonis*, l. 5.
7. *Titus Andronicus* II, 3
8. *Timon of Athens* I, 2.
9. *Troilus and Cressida* IV, 4.
10. *Lover's Complaint*, l. 18.
11. *Macbeth* II, 1.

accepit solitam flammam[9] lectumque iugalem:[10]
"O virgo, nova mi facies,[11] gratissima coniunx,[12]
venisti tandem,[13] mea sola et sera voluptas.[14]
o dulcis coniunx, non haec sine numine divum[15]
proveniunt:[16] placitone etiam pugnabis amori?"[17]

  Talia dicentem iamdudum aversa tuetur[18]
cunctaturque metu telumque instare tremiscit[19]
spemque metumque inter[20] funditque has ore
      loquelas:[21]
"Per te, per, qui te talem genuere, parentes,[22]
o formose puer,[23] noctem non amplius unam[24]
hanc tu, oro, solare inopem[25] et miserere precantis.[26]
succidimus: non lingua valet, non corpore notae
sufficiunt vires, nec vox aut verba sequuntur."[27]

9. *Aen.* viii. 388.
10. *Aen.* iv. 496.
11. *Aen.* vi. 104.
12. *Aen.* x. 607.
13. *Aen.* vi. 687.
14. *Aen.* viii. 581.
15. *Aen.* ii. 777.
16. *Aen.* xii. 428.
17. *Aen.* iv. 38.
18. *Aen.* iv. 362.
19. *Aen.* xii. 916.
20. *Aen.* i. 218.
21. *Aen.* v. 842.
22. *Aen.* x. 597.
23. *Ecl.* ii. 17.
24. *Aen.* i. 683.
25. *Aen.* ix. 290.
26. *Aen.* x. 598.
27. *Aen.* xii. 911.

Now kiss, embrace, contend, do what you will.[12]
He doth embrace and hug.[13] Sir, in. Very good.
Well kissed! An excellent courtesy.[14] Cry, "O
sweet creature!"[15] Look to it![16] Is she not a modest
    young lady?[17]
Her affability and bashful modesty[18]
'gainst his fierce blaze of riot cannot last.[19]
What nature teaches beasts[20] and the burning eyes
of heaven[21] dare look on,[22] they will do, and do[23]
with like timorous accent and dire yell[24]
in the honor of their parents'[25] gentle exercise[26]
by which they were begun and well begot.[27]
She now begs[28] some little time.[29] "Wait I beseech
    you . . .[30]
The more delay'd delighted. Be content."[31]

12. *Two Gentlemen of Verona* I, 2.
13. *Timon of Athens* I, 1.
14. *Othello* II, 1.
15. *Othello* III, 3.
16. *As You Like It* III, 1.
17. *Much Ado About Nothing* I, 1.
18. *Taming of the Shrew* II, 1.
19. *Richard II* II, 1.
20. *Coriolanus* II, 1.
21. *Hamlet* II, 2.
22. *Macbeth* III, 4.
23. *Macbeth* I, 3.
24. *Othello* I, 1.
25. *Winter's Tale* I, 2.
26. *1st part Henry IV* V, 2.
27. *As You Like It* V, 4.
28. *Henry VIII* III, 1.
29. *Hamlet* II, 2.
30. *Romeo and Juliet* I, 3.
31. *Cymbeline* V, 4.

ille autem: "Causas nequiquam nectis inanes,"[28]
praecipitatque moras omnis[29] solvitque pudorem.[30]

Parecbasis

Hactenus castis auribus audiendum mysterium nuptiale
ambitu loquendi et circuitione velavi. verum quoniam
et Fescenninos amat celebritas nuptialis verborumque
petulantiam notus vetere instituto ludus admittit, cetera
quoque cubiculi et lectuli operta prodentur ab eodem
auctore collecta, ut bis erubescamus, qui et Vergilium
faciamus impudentem. vos, si placet, hic iam legendi
modum ponite: cetera curiosis relinquite.

28. *Aen.* ix. 219.
29. *Aen.* xii. 699.
30. *Aen.* iv. 55.

"Nay, answer me. Stand and unfold yourself."[32]
"I will satisfy you, if ever I satisfied man."[33]

Parecbasis: The Surgeon General's Warning

Thus far, it's a parlor game. But the bounds of good taste have no place here. Prudes and sissies, this is where you'll want to stop. Sex is a serious business, and so, for that matter, is literature. What Ausonius did with old Virge (Parthenias, they used to call him), I can do with the immoral bawd of Avon. And because the Loeb library leaves the lewd text untranslated, I feel obliged to press on. In a spirit of public service, peut-être? Or sheer perversity. (Perverts have rights, too, after all.) Think of it this way: I could have been using as my source text . . . The Bible! As Brother Dave Gardner used to say, that Good Book is a very good book indeed. You can hear the people in motels who are, presumably, reading their Gideons late on Saturday nights as they cry out in delight and joy, "Oh, God, oh, God, it's good!"

32. *Hamlet* I, 1.
33. *As You Like It* V, 2.

VIII
Imminutio

Postquam congressi[1] sola sub nocte per umbram[2]
et mentem Venus ipsa dedit,[3] nova proelia temptant.[4]
tollit se arrectum:[5] conantem plurima frustra[6]
occupat os faciemque,[7] pedem pede fervidus urget,[8]
perfidus alta petens:[9] ramum, qui veste latebat,[10]
sanguineis ebuli bacis minioque rubentem[11]
nudato capite[12] et pedibus per mutua nexis,[13]
monstrum horrendum, informe, ingens, cui lumen
    ademptum,[14]
eripit a femore et trepidanti fervidus instat.[15]

1. *Aen.* xi. 631.
2. *Aen.* vi. 268.
3. *Georg.* iii. 267.
4. *Aen.* iii. 240.
5. *Aen.* x. 892.
6. *Aen.* ix. 398.
7. *Aen.* x. 699.
8. *Aen.* xii. 748.
9. *Aen.* vii. 362.
10. *Aen.* vi. 406.
11. *Ecl.* x. 27.
12. *Aen.* xii. 312.
13. *Aen.* vii. 66.
14. *Aen.* iii. 658.
15. *Aen.* x. 788.

VIII
The Bumping of the Uglies

What do you here alone?[1] O God of battles!

steel their soldiers' hearts.[2] His purity

of manhood stands upright,[3] whose dreadful sword

was never drawn in vain.[4] "Naked as I am,

I will assault thee."[5] Look down.[6] The purple pride,[7]

and jewels, two stones, two rich and precious

      stones . . .[8]

They are dangerous weapons for maids.[9] She takes the

      staff

in her mouth and guides it,[10] that his puissance holds.[11]

The hand's more instrumental than the mouth.[12]

Of all thy sex, most monster like,[13] one eye

1. *Othello* III, 3.
2. *Henry V* IV, 1.
3. *Timon of Athens* IV, 3.
4. *2nd part Henry IV* IV, 1.
5. *Othello* V, 2.
6. *Winter's Tale* III, 2.
7. Sonnet XCIX.
8. *Merchant of Venice* II, 8.
9. *Much Ado About Nothing* V, 2.
10. *Titus Andronicus* IV, 1.
11. *2nd part Henry VI* IV, 2.
12. *Hamlet* I, 2.
13. *Antony and Cleopatra* IV, 12.

est in secessu,[16] tenuis quo semita ducit,[17]
ignea rima micans:[18] exhalat opaca mephitim.[19]
nulli fas casto sceleratum insistere limen.[20]
hic specus horrendum:[21] talis sese halitus atris
faucibus effundens[22] nares contingit odore.[23]
huc iuvenis nota fertur regione viarum[24]
et super incumbens[25] nodis et cortice crudo
intorquet summis adnixus viribus hastam.[26]
haesit virgineumque alte bibit acta cruorem.[27]
insonuere cavae gemitumque dedere cavernae.[28]
illa manu moriens telum trahit, ossa sed inter[29]
altius ad vivum persedit[30] vulnere mucro.[31]
ter sese attollens cubitoque innixa levavit,

16. *Aen.* i. 159.
17. *Aen.* xi. 524.
18. *Aen.* viii. 392.
19. *Aen.* vii. 84.
20. *Aen.* vi. 563.
21. *Aen.* vii. 568.
22. *Aen.* vi. 240f.
23. *Aen.* vii. 480.
24. *Aen.* xi. 530.
25. *Aen.* v. 858.
26. *Aen.* ix. 743f.
27. *Aen.* xi. 804.
28. *Aen.* ii. 53.
29. *Aen.* xi. 816.
30. *Georg.* iii. 442.
31. *Aen.* xi. 817.

thou hast to look to heaven for grace.[14] The doors,
being shut against his entrance,[15] with instruments
upon them fit to open,[16] be the ram
to batter[17] such an ivory wall.[18] Are ye
undone? No, ye fat chuffs. On bacons, on![19]
The ruddiness upon her lip is wet.[20]
Not an inch further?[21] He sticks deeper, grows
with more pernicious root[22] to shake the bags[23]
and make the coming hour o'erflow with joy
and pleasure drown the brim,[24] for one to thrust,
his hand between his teeth.[25] And mark the moan
she makes.[26] Most resolutely snatched,[27] he is
far gone, far gone,[28] to the profoundest pit,[29]

14. *1st part Henry VI* I, 4.
15. *Comedy of Errors* IV, 3.
16. *Romeo and Juliet* V, 3.
17. *Antony and Cleopatra* III, 2.
18. *Rape of Lucrece*, l. 464.
19. *1st part Henry IV* II, 2.
20. *Winter's Tale* V, 3.
21. *1st part Henry IV* II, 3.
22. *Macbeth* IV, 3.
23. *King John* III, 3.
24. *All's Well That Ends Well* II, 4.
25. *3rd part Henry VI* I, 4.
26. *Two Gentlemen of Verona* II, 3
27. *1st part Henry IV* I, 2.
28. *Hamlet* II, 2.
29. *Hamlet* IV, 5.

ter revoluta toro est.[32] manet imperterritus ille.[33]
nec mora nec requies:[34] clavumque adfixus et haerens
nusquam amittebat oculosque sub astra tenebat.[35]
itque reditque viam totiens[36] uteroque recusso[37]
transadigit costas[38] et pectine pulsat eburno.[39]
iamque fere spatio extremo fessique sub ipsam
finem adventabant:[40] tum creber anhelitus artus
aridaque ora quatit, sudor fluit undique rivis,[41]
labitur exanguis,[42] destillat ab inguine virus.[43]

> Contentus esto, Paule mi,
> lasciva, Paule, pagina:
> ridere, nil ultra, expeto.

32. *Aen.* iv. 690.
33. *Aen.* x. 770.
34. *Georg.* iii. 110.
35. *Aen.* v. 852f.
36. *Aen.* vi. 122.
37. *Aen.* ii. 52.
38. *Aen.* xii. 276.
39. *Aen.* vi. 647.
40. *Aen.* v. 327f.
41. *Aen.* v. 199f.
42. *Aen.* xi. 818.
43. *Georg.* iii. 281.

where the dribbling dart of love[30] doth melt and
    pour[31]
froth and scum,[32] hot and full,[33] to shake
their frames,[34] his hair uprear'd, his nostrils stretch'd
with struggling.[35] Look on the sheets, his hair, you see
is sticking.[36] But soft! See how busily she turns.[37]
He doth revive again: madam, be patient.[38]
Why these balls bound. There's noise in it. 'Tis hard[39]
And will he not come again?[40] Spit, fire! Spout, rain![41]

Here follow a score or so of lines of beetling prose by
way of justification, apology, and appeals to precedent
that never do any good, because prudes will find a way
to put you down no matter how you try to head them
off at the pass. Poor Ausonius! He says, quite truthfully,
that it's all from Virgil, although he knows that only
makes his performance all the more deplorable. And
that, in any event, this is what happens at weddings, isn't

30. *Measure for Measure* I, 3.
31. *Antony and Cleopatra* II, 5.
32. *Merry Wives of Windsor* I, 1.
33. *Hamlet* I, 1.
34. *Measure for Measure* II, 4.
35. *2nd part Henry VI* III, 2.
36. *2nd part Henry VI* III, 2.
37. *Titus Andronicus* IV, 1.
38. *2nd part Henry VI* III, 2.
39. *All's Well that Ends Well* II, 3.
40. *Hamlet* IV, 5.
41. *King Lear* III, 2.

it? (The appeal to nature is as desperate as the appeal to reason and taste.) What he should have said is that a dirty mind is a great comfort, and that if the devil can cite scripture to his purpose, at least he can take credit for having read some.

SELECTED EPIGRAMS

XXV

Here, read, by morning light or lamplight,
my pages, bright or somber, as life is too.
Let each piece find its right reader and moment:
Venus may bless this verse and Minerva that;
the stoic may nod in agreement here, while there
the epicure approves.
                              But let us agree
to tolerate one another, observing good manners,
and the serious Muse may allow me my little jokes.

IV

Dr. Quack's prognosis: dire—
that Gaius would forthwith expire.
He did, indeed, but then, though dead,
returned to the world.
                              And the doctor said,
"Gaius? You? Are you back again?"
"I am sent," said the ghost, "to the world of men

on behalf of my master, Dis, who is ill
and needs a physician to give him a pill . . ."
Quack went abruptly pale and cold
to hear such news, whereupon his old
patient laughed: "I'm unlikely to pick
on your help again for one who's sick."

V

You caw or neigh,
bleat or bray,
crow or bay,
cluck or squeak,
or quack . . . With any word you say
you betray yourself. You start to speak
and it's a barnyard.
Magnifique!

IX

That bust of Rufinus? Him to the life! How come?
No tongue, no brain, blind, stiff, and utterly dumb . . .
To every aspect of him does this piece conform, or
almost. He was perhaps a little warmer.

LXXXIX

Give me a mistress cute and pert,
quick to quarrel, and common as dirt,
not too truthful, moody, vain,
an exquisite balance of pleasure and pain.
Otherwise, if she be good,
modest, always cheerful in mood,
and an ornament to any man's life,
I'm apt to want her to be my wife.

LIX

"With only three guys in bed, I put it to you,
there are two insert-ors, as they say, and two insert-ees.
How?"
                    "A riddle! Give me a moment, please.
But that's four, with two being done and two who do!"
"The middle fellow is busy; he counts as two."

CIV

No, Apollo, no,
throw down that bow
and drop your enormous quiver.
It isn't from you that Daphne runs. Her shiver
of fear, during this pursuit,
is for all those darts you'd shoot,
and what, if she stood, you'd deliver.

XXXVIII

Myron, you old goat, I'm afraid
the chances of your getting laid
grow slimmer. Laïs said no, but you
blackened your gray hair with goo
from a barber's bottle and tried again.
She turned you down again, but then,
making worse what was already bad,
added, "Give my regards to your dad."

XL

O wife of mine, we've done okay.
Let's just keep going on this way.
You're my cutie; I'm your bear.
I dance for you in my underwear
still, like a kid. If I should get
to Nestor's age, and you, my pet,
are old as the Sibyl of Cumae,
we'll give the calendar the lie.

What is time worth? Who can tell
unless, like us, they spend it well?

LXXX

Marcus' condition is very grave
(the soothsayer gives him maybe a week),
so he calls on Dr. Alcon: "Save
my life! And show that other guy
to be a fake."
                    "Well, I will try."
Does Alcon's treatment do the trick?
Alas, poor Marcus, I report,
expires that evening, six days short.

LXXXVIII

Ah, curly-girl, they say you're funny looking?
I don't agree.
But as I'm the jealous type (and what lover isn't?)
I like it if you look a little funny to them.
You look great to me!

LXIV

In Sparta once, Minerva met
Venus in armor, cap a pie.
"Let us contend again, and let
Paris be judge," said she.

"Indeed," answered Venus, "but first I trust
you'll give me a moment or two to prepare?
In order to fight at my best I must
get out of these clothes and go bare."

LVII

Grace, whenever she's at dances,
clumps about and shuffles so.
Does her sister Prudence take risky chances?
Or her sister Honor ever say "No"?

About the Translator

David R. Slavitt was educated at Andover and Yale and has published more than sixty books: original poetry (recently *PS3569.L3*), translations (recently *Broken Columns*, of Statius and Claudian), novels (recently *The Cliff*), critical works (recently *Virgil*), and short stories. He worked for seven years as a journalist at *Newsweek* and continues to do freelance reporting and reviewing. He is coeditor, with Palmer Bovie, of the Penn Greek Drama Series.

Printed in the United Kingdom
by Lightning Source UK Ltd.
110499UKS00001B/82